C000234804

DON'TS
FOR DANCERS

DON'TS
FOR DANCERS

BY

KARSINOVA

LONDON
A. & C. BLACK, LTD.
1925

Published September, 1925.

And here is my first:

As long as the breath of life is in you, *don't* ever miss the chance of a dance— up on your feet and keep dancing as long as the music lasts!

KARSINOVA.

DON'TS FOR DANCERS

1.—DON'TS FOR THE DIFFIDENT.

DON'T imagine you will never make a dancer because you are by nature clumsy. Dancing will cure you. It will train you to move and hold yourself gracefully. It will conquer your self-consciousness.

Don't say you are too tired to dance because you have had a tiring day. Your mind and your muscles need change of exercise, and dancing gives you this in a happy atmosphere. The exhilaration of the music and the stimulus of your fellow-dancers' society will make you forget that you are fagged out.

Don't say you can't afford to dance although you love it. Try. Economise on something less healthful. You will find it worth while.

Don't stay away from a dance because you happen to be feeling glum. Don't look glum, that's all. Dancing will cure any ordinary fit of the blues.

Don't be too shy to dance. You will be surprised, once you have taken the plunge, how quickly the shyness wears off.

Don't miss an opportunity of making converts if you yourself are keen on dancing. Infuse your friends with your own enthusiasm. They will be grateful to you presently, you may be sure, for dancing is a wonderful tonic.

Don't say your dancing days are done. Your dancing days are never done until you are confined to a bath chair for exercise. If you can walk to the office in the morning and play a game of golf on Sundays, there is no reason why you shouldn't foot it with the best every night of the week. A man is only as old as he feels, and, under proper conditions, dancing is such a wonderful rejuvenator that there is no reason why anyone should feel old at all. Moreover, don't forget dancing is a splendid anti-fat. It will cure that middle-aged spread you are getting so alarmed about.

II.—DRESS.

Don't wear clothes that are tight.

"Let joy be unconfined!"

Perfect freedom of movement is absolutely essential to graceful dancing. Besides, tight clothes are so heating.

Don't wear shoes that are even the least bit small for you. Better that your feet should appear a trifle longer than they really are than that they should be uncomfortable. On the other hand—

Don't wear shoes that are too large for you. Shoes that slip up and down will spoil your dancing, and give you blisters and even corns!

Don't wear stockings or socks that are too short in the foot—a frequent cause of enlarged toe-joints, as any foot expert will tell you.

Don't economise on your shoes and stockings, but buy the very best you can afford. Save on your dress, rather than on your footgear. This will repay you both in appearance and in comfort.

Don't wear stockings or socks of which the feet have been badly darned. A rough, clumsy darn may cause you as much foot discomfort as a badly finished shoe.

Don't put on your stockings hurriedly and carelessly. See first that the feet fit perfectly, then take care that the seam at the back is straight. A crooked stocking-seam will spoil your whole appearance, no matter how smart your dress may be.

Don't buy your stockings in a hurry. If you have decided on the fashionable flesh-coloured kind, take care you don't select too vivid a pink. This is most unbecoming to your ankles.

Don't wear gloves. These were discarded during the war, and though attempts are being made in certain quarters to restore them to favour, the fashion has not caught on again up to the present. Just as well, perhaps, in view of our diminished incomes.

Don't wear a black waistcoat or a black tie with full evening dress.

Don't wear a dinner-jacket—for which a black waistcoat and black tie are *de rigueur*—except for a very informal dance.

Don't wear a made-up tie on any occasion whatsoever. This is always, and under any circumstances, an abomination.

Don't wear coloured socks with evening dress.

Don't use strong, cheap scent or strongly scented powder. It is very bad form. The merest breath of some delicate perfume is charming and quite permissible, but a pungent, heavy odour is nauseating. Most men dislike a partner who simply reeks of scent.

Don't use ordinary pins on any portion of your dress. Sooner or later, in the course of the evening, they will probably stick into you. Or your partner may find them out. Remember, a pin-scratch can lead to ugly consequences. And if you must use safety-pins, let them be good, reliable ones, of the flat-fastening kind.

Don't forget to slip one or two emergency safety-pins and a needle and cotton into your vanity-bag, in case of need.

Don't wear a collar that is either too high or too tight. If it were "done," a tennis shirt with open throat would be the ideal thing. But as it isn't done, try and find a collar which, while conforming to convention, does not impede the free movement of your head.

Don't overload yourself with jewellery, particularly with dangling pen-

dants or strings of beads that are
liable to float around as you dance and
catch in other people's dress.

Don't choose an *outré* or conspicuous
dance-frock, however smart, if you
can't afford many new ones. A dress
in which you will have to appear again
and again had better not be too
striking, lest it become hopelessly
dated. The latest "extreme" is for
the chosen few who can discard their
clothes with every whim of fashion.

Don't be unhappy because you are
wearing an old frock. Remember that
it is not so old to other people as it is
to you. *You* may think it shabby,

but you are invariably more critical than they. And it isn't your frock, but the way you dance, that matters to your partner.

III.—FANCY DRESS.

Don't wear fancy costumes that are completely foreign to your appearance and personality, unless you are endeavouring to amuse the children. For instance:

Don't disguise yourself as "Lohengrin" if you happen to be short and stout. This sort of thing is excusable only in an operatic tenor.

Don't choose a Harlequin's tights unless you are quite sure that your figure is beyond reproach.

Don't aspire to be a Columbine unless your knees may safely challenge comparison, say, with Pavlova's.

Don't wear any costume, no matter how effective, that handicaps your dancing.

Don't, for instance, go to a carnival ball disguised as a pillar-box. It may make other people laugh, but you will spend a miserable evening. Or if someone offers to lend you a perfect suit of armour, don't succumb to the temptation to wear it, even if it fits. No doubt you will look splendid in it —but you will want to lie down most of the time.

Don't wear the kind of get-up that is a nuisance to other dancers. If you are tall and slender, it may occur to you to represent a Maypole—nosegay,

green wreath, and gaily fluttering
ribbons—very charming, yes! But
those ribbons have a trick of fluttering
gaily where they are not wanted.
Think twice before you make up your
mind!

IV.—FITNESS.

Don't eat a heavy, indigestible meal immediately before the dance. No one is young enough to do this with impunity. And, at the best, it will make you lazy.

Don't dance in a stuffy, ill-ventilated room, if you can avoid it. Dancing, like any other healthy exercise, makes a demand for an increased action of the heart and respiratory organs. If there is a plentiful supply of fresh air, you will benefit by the exercise and have no "fagged-out" feeling the following morning.

Don't sit in a draught or in the open air between dances until you feel chilly. Cool down by all means, but don't use less sense towards yourself or your partner than you would towards your horse or motor-bike.

Don't cut dances for the card-room and buffet, or, if you do, don't blame the dance for that jaded feeling next morning.

Don't drink large quantities of lemonade or any other liquid if dancing is apt to make you too hot.

Don't allow yourself to grow hot and sticky. In modern ballroom dancing there is no dance sufficiently strenuous to excuse a streaming forehead. It merely indicates that you are badly out of condition and need more exercise. The old-fashioned dances no doubt demanded fresh collars for the gentlemen at frequent intervals, but should such a thing be necessary, remember it is not a thing to boast of nowadays.

Don't allow yourself to stiffen up in the joints and muscles. A few simple exercises, such as rising slowly on the toes, bending and stretching the knees, etc., if practised for five minutes night and morning, will keep you more or less in good training as far as ballroom dancing is concerned.

Don't be a martyr to your feet. Many dancers at the beginning of the season have their evening's enjoyment completely ruined by foot discomfort. A little talcum powder dusted on the soles of your feet will do much to remedy that burning feeling. Another excellent preventative measure is to dab the soles every night with a piece of cotton-wool soaked in methylated spirits. If this is done for a week or so before the dancing season starts you will be quite free from discomfort.

Don't go to a dance when you are suffering from a cold in the head. Much better cancel your engagement and retire to bed. Even if you are not feeling particularly bad, your presence at the dance is a menace to others.

V.—PITFALLS BIG AND LITTLE.

Don't make the mistake of thinking you can learn to dance by merely watching people's feet and "picking up the steps," unless you are a born dancer. And born dancers are rare.

Don't grudge paying for lessons. A good teacher is worth his fee.

Don't take these lessons haphazard from some "professor" of whose credentials you know nothing. Slipshod and faulty methods of instruction take a lot of counteracting. As with everything else, so with dancing: bad habits, once acquired, are difficult to unlearn.

Don't dance before you know how to walk and hold yourself properly. Bear in mind that poise and balance are essential to graceful dancing.

To Walk Well.

Don't hold yourself rigidly, but stand quite naturally, with a straight back and chest expanded.

Don't hunch up your shoulders.

Don't thrust out your chin.

Don't keep your head down.

Don't stiffen your arms.

Don't push out your elbows.

Don't move from the knees, but from the hips.

To Bow Gracefully.

Don't jerk your head, but bend it slowly.

Don't bend the body more than is necessary to make the line from head to waist a graceful curve.

Don't be stiff.   Allow the hands and arms to hang loosely.

GENTLEMEN:

Don't offer your hand to your partner palm downwards.   Remember it is the lady who places her hand in yours. Don't grip it tightly, but let your thumb close gently over it.

Don't hold your partner tightly round the waist, thereby restricting her movements. Remember that perfect freedom of the hips is essential to graceful dancing. Place your right hand well above her waist.

Don't grip your partner's hand as in a death-grapple. The hands need do no more than support each other.

Don't hold your partner *too* loosely, or you cannot steer her. But bear in mind that the gentlest possible pressure of the guiding hand should be sufficient.

Don't guide forcibly, for this is upsetting to the balance. Guidance, in fact, should be almost as much mental as physical.

Don't stretch out your left arm like a pump-handle. It is not only ungainly, but dangerous to other dancers.

Don't raise your partner's arm above the level of her shoulders. This forces her into an uncomfortable and ungraceful position.

Don't take too long steps. It is not only ungraceful, but selfish. Remember that your partner's step is naturally shorter than yours—unless she happens to be taller than you are. Adapt your step to hers.

Don't forget that it is up to you to study your partner's little idiosyncrasies and to give way to them as far as lies in your power.

LADIES:

Don't try to guide your partner. Leave everything to him. If you try to act on your own, the result will be confusion. Respond to his guidance automatically. He will take full responsibility for steering your course and setting the step.

Don't hold on to your partner's arm with your left hand. Place it lightly on his shoulder. This will give you all the support you need.

Don't let your hair stray unduly.
Contrary to what the novelists would
have us believe, it irritates a man
intensely to have a wisp of your hair
sweeping across his face. So, keep
your locks in order!

Don'ts for Both.

Don't straddle. Besides being ungainly, straddling makes guidance
almost an impossibility. Try to keep
the feet more or less in line.

Don't get into the middle of the
floor. Always keep going with the
crowd and preserve an imaginary
boundary line on the inside of the
circuit.

Don't dance with your tongue between your teeth. This may seem an absurd admonition; but I have seen novices, as in elementary writing lessons, performing the intricacies of the dance with their tongues. A stumble, or a collision, and the "lapsing lingua" is badly bitten!

Don't be afraid to practise. Practise wherever you get an opportunity, at classes or in private. It is only in this way you will attain perfection of style.

Don't learn to waltz one way only. Practise reversing from the very beginning, and you will find it far easier than

if you got into the way of dancing
forward only.

Don't imagine that when you have
learnt the steps of a dance, you have
learnt everything.   Don't be satisfied
until you have gained such perfect
mastery over the mere mechanics of a
dance that you can forget your feet
completely and give yourself up to the
sheer joy of movement and rhythm.

Don't, when passing one foot in
front of or behind the other, raise it as
though you were about to kick some
object.   Keep your toes pointing
downwards, and glide rather than lift
the foot.   Except in some very special
cases, the impression upon the on-

looker should be that your feet never really leave the ground.

Don't dance with bent knees. Bent knees suggest an ancient cab-horse on its last pathetic stagger or a performing chimpanzee gyrating round its keeper. The knees should be ready to bend when necessary, but most of the actual "play" should come from the ankle and the ball of the foot.

Don't roll and lurch like a ship in a heavy swell. Move gracefully to the music. Any exaggerated swaying is ungraceful, and grace and ease are the two things most essential to a perfect style.

Don't hitch your shoulders up and down. Some ungainly dancers jerk their shoulders in such a manner as to suggest some chronic irritation at the base of the shoulder-blades. Let your shoulders look after themselves. If the lilt of the music is in your toes, your shoulders will follow of their own accord.

Don't keep your eyes on the floor. The moment you begin watching your feet, or those of your partner, you lose your poise. And that lost, all is lost.

Don't turn in your toes when doing the backward step of the waltz. You will probably find you have a tendency to do this, and it looks far from graceful.

Don't lean on your partner. Hold your body erect, but not rigid.

Don't forget to keep all the weight of your body on the inside or pivot foot when turning.

Don't expect to become an expert waltzer after half a dozen lessons or a week's practice at a Palais de Danse. You can go on perfecting yourself almost indefinitely.

Don't pick up grotesque and ugly variations of a dance for the sake of their novelty, or because they are easier to learn than the correct style.

Don't omit to count to yourself all the time when you are learning. It is the easiest way to overcome the difficulties of any step. Learn to count correctly, and you have the step. But don't count your steps out loud; it is most irritating to your partner. Until you are able to do a step without counting it, don't do that step in public. Try one you do know.

Don't attempt the "Jazz-Step" in public until you have thoroughly mastered it in private. It is apt to look ungainly and ridiculous when badly done, but you can attain to grace with practice, and it will be worth the trouble.

Don't be intimidated by the Tango. Don't lose heart because you know you will never learn all the steps you have seen experts dance. They will tell you that there are hundreds. But don't let that prevent your enjoying half a dozen. They will suffice. The acrobatic Tango is out of place in a ballroom, anyway.

Don't be tempted, when you are proficient, to indulge in vulgar burlesques of the accredited steps. Don't give the Stigginses another handle.

Don't forget that hopping is bad form in any dance, except the Schottische and its first cousin, the Highland Schottische.

Don't romp through the figures of a square dance, but keep strict time to the music.

Don't join in a square dance if you have not danced it for years and can't remember the figures properly. You will cause confusion in your set, and spoil the enjoyment of the other dancers as well as your own.

Don't say to yourself you can't practise because you have no partner to practise with. Turn on the gramophone and practise by yourself. If you have no gramophone, hum a little tune, or whistle—make music of some kind for the sake of the rhythm.

Don't forget that it is this sense of rhythm, the feeling for music, that will enable you to move in harmony with it, that will make you dance.

Don't run away with the idea that style in dancing is something a person is born with and cannot be acquired. It can be acquired if you are willing to take the necessary trouble.

Don't be angular, that is the main point to bear in mind.   Cultivate curves.   Let your joints be flexible. Smoothness of carriage is more than half the secret of graceful dancing. Avoid all crude angles and smoothness will follow automatically.

Don't form a right-angle with your foot and ankle. Point the toe downwards.

Don't form a straight line with your arm. Let it bend at wrist and elbow.

Don't hold your partner's hand with stiff fingers. Bend them lightly.

Don't bow as though you suffered from stiffening of the joints. Hold yourself loosely and naturally, and let your joints have full play. Curves, not angles, please remember.

Don't be obsessed by the notion that you can only dance with certain partners whose step happens to suit yours. Make up your mind that you can adapt yourself to most partners and you will find that you can.

Don't be afraid of unknown partners. If you expect difficulties, your mind will be sure to react on your body and difficulties will arise. Have confidence and the difficulties will vanish.

VI.—MANNERS AND MORALS.

For the Expert.

Don't show off. You may make your partner's life a misery by insisting on complicated steps which she is unable to follow.

Don't lose your temper if you find your partner is not the ideal dancer. Should he, or she, be timid and inexperienced, be content with simple steps.

Don't get mad if your partner gets out of step occasionally. These little things must not be taken seriously.

After all, you are there to enjoy your-selves.

Don't put on supercilious airs if you find yourself at a gathering where the old-fashioned square dances are popular. Join in the fun and appear to like it, even if you don't.

Don't allow your partner to see that you are not quite happy with her. If she is a bad dancer, don't make her a worse one by betraying your feelings. Don't suggest an ice or a breath of air on the balcony half-way through the dance. She will see through your motive and be miserable.

Don't behave like an instructor. Don't keep on telling her what she

ought to do. It will only worry her
and make her nervous, and will do *you*
no good. Simplify your step as much
as possible to suit her limitations.
If you can possibly manage it, behave
as though you were enjoying yourself.

Don't betray your superiority if
you are an adept at fox-trotting and
your partner knows only a single
step. Don't hint that his step is
monotonous. Put up with it for the
sake of his feelings.

Don't volunteer criticism, but if you
are asked for it, don't be afraid to give
it—tactfully, of course, without dis-
couraging the diffident, and in such
a way that it will be helpful.

Don't put him, or her, off with insincere protestations, but take a little trouble and you will find your partner grateful and ready to profit by your hints.

Don't use technical terms when asked to explain a step to anybody. Technical terms are very excellent for textbooks but quite unnecessary when a practical demonstration can be given.

FOR THE NOVICE.

Don't arrive at a dance too early. A silent, empty ballroom is not a cheerful place, and the highest spirits are apt to be damped by hanging around.

Don't be casual towards your hostess at a private dance. Make your bow to her as soon after arriving as circumstances will permit, and on no account neglect to bid her good-night on departing.

Don't imagine you are the cynosure of all eyes and allow yourself to become nervous and self-conscious. Remember that the other dancers are not there to criticise you, but to enjoy themselves. Dancing is a relaxation, you know, and not a task. Self-consciousness and relaxation are impossible partners.

Don't jump to the conclusion, if you hear a laugh, that the laugh is at your

expense, or take it for granted, should
you intercept a smile, that people are
making fun of you. You are not as
conspicuous as you imagine.

Don't let some little misadventure
spoil your evening. If you have come
a cropper, be ready to laugh at yourself.
To betray temper or mortification will
make you look ridiculous and be
remembered when otherwise your
mishap would have been forgotten the
next moment.

Don't join a strange dance-club
before you have found out something
about it. Dance-clubs of the right
sort are excellent institutions and will
afford you great pleasure and recreation

at a moderate costs but—there are dance-clubs *and* dance -clubs.

Don't be afraid of confessing your ignorance. It is much better to say frankly that you can only do the most elementary dance-steps than to stumble through a maze of intricacies you know nothing about. Your partner will be grateful.

Don't be frightened of your partner. After all, it takes two to make a dance, and getting flustered never did anybody any good. Your partner will find it much easier to help you if you take things easy.

For Everybody.

Don't be afraid of being the first couple on the floor. Someone has to make a start, and the other dancers are much too occupied with their own partners to notice you and yours.

Don't wait until the music is half over before you begin to dance. Nothing is more exasperating to your partner, if she is a keen dancer, than this habit of dallying away the precious moments.

Don't talk. It is impossible to dance well and keep up a constant flow of conversation at the same time. Try to feel only the lilt of the music, the swing and rhythm of it, for that is the secret of perfect dancing.

Don't grouse at the band, even if it is not up to the level of Jack Hylton's. Make the best of it. Don't blame the music every time you get out of step. This will only irritate your partner and help you not at all.

Don't use your partner as a battering-ram in order to force a passage through a congested corner of the ballroom. The first duty of every dancer is to avoid collisions.

Don't cut across other couples unless there is a clear space. There is nothing more annoying to the other dancers,

and the number of apologies you will
have to make quite minimises any
advantage the cut may have appeared
to offer.

Don't keep on drawing unfavourable
comparisons between this dance and
the last one you were at—with a
different partner.   Don't harp upon
how much you enjoyed that one—how
divinely *he*, or she, danced—how
perfect everything had been.   It will
not make the present more delightful.

Don't look worried to death over the
dance.   Dancing is, and has been from
time   immemorial,   an   expression   of
joy.   Even if you are English, don't
take your pleasures *too* sadly.

Don't glare angrily if another couple should chance to bump you. Even if it is entirely the others' fault, they may not know it. A polite "Sorry" and a smile will do more to add to the evening's enjoyment than will the unnecessary frown.

Don't, should you and your partner be particularly well suited, succumb to the temptation to show off. Leave exhibition dancing to those who make their living thereby. That is not to say you must never indulge in new steps with your partner, for this would greatly diminish the interest of dancing. But remember that to make yourself conspicuous is to invite unfavourable criticism.

Don't be unreasonable in your demand for encores. Over-appreciation is only a polite word for greed, and though the gentlemen of the orchestra are human enough to feel gratified by your applause, they are also subject to human limitations.

Don't criticise your late partner too candidly. You may be talking to some friend or relation. Names are so confusing and difficult to catch.

Don't be noisy. The breezy, boisterous dancer who howls the choruses of all the popular fox-trots is a horrible nuisance to his partner and everybody else.

Don't, if you are in some out-of-the way corner, turn up your nose if the dances are not quite those you dance in your own circle. Join in the fun, and you'll find that any dances are better than none. Besides, you are sure to find someone who can pick up your steps quite easily as long as you don't adopt a supercilious attitude.

Don't cut dances. When you have filled your programme, abide by it. There is no excuse, short of illness or sudden calamity, for such absolute rudeness.

Don't be jealous if your particular partner is, for the time being, dancing with somebody else. This may seem a somewhat personal admonition, but I have suffered from the kind of partner whose attention, from the moment the dance began, was riveted upon another couple. It was most uncomfortable for me, I assure you.

Don't fail to preserve your sense of humour. There are many occasions in the ballroom when this will stand you in good stead. On the other hand—

Don't always be making other dancers a target for your wit, however comic they may appear to you, unless you are prepared to be laughed at yourself. There are funny sights, we know, and a sense of the ridiculous is a happy gift, but the man who is for ever trying to see the absurdity of others is a perfect nuisance.

Don't argue with your partner about the correctness of this or that step. Give way gracefully even if you know you are right. After all, what *does* it matter?

Don't attach undue importance to the fact that Jill is always dancing with Jack. You need not feel either unduly depressed or unduly elated, from a sentimental point of view. Remember that the modern dancing partner is an accepted fact and not an accepted affinity. So don't worry—find someone to match your step and— keep dancing.

Don't be shy about calling your partner's attention to a smut on his nose or a tear in her frock. The kind thing is to point it out before other people have noticed it too.

Don't sulk if you can't get the partner you want. There are as good fish in the sea as ever came out of it, and—who knows?—the plain girl in the dowdy frock may be an exquisite dancer. Anyway, she'll dance all the better if you give her your undivided attention.

Don't express your precise feelings if your partner should be unlucky enough to tear your frock. Be a sport. Remember there are worse disasters in

the world than a damaged dress, and
he is probably far more miserable
about it than you are. This is your
chance of showing a little unselfish-
ness.

Don't complain of aches and pains
to your partner. If you are not in a
fit state of health to enjoy the dance,
don't go. But if you *must* go, don't
spoil other people's pleasure.

Don't be too enthusiastic about some
other girl present. Loud and frequently
expressed admiration of that other
one's wonderful dancing or of her
exquisite frock may easily be inter-
preted by your own partner as dis-
paragement of herself.

Don't make yourself and your partner conspicuous either by your method of dressing or of dancing. Attracting attention and attracting admiration are not always the same thing, you know.

Don't insist on Bostoning or Hesitating if your partner loves the conventional waltz. And, conversely, don't stress the older form if she has expressed her preference for the Boston or Hesitation.

Don't introduce eccentricities into your dance which might be taken exception to either by your partner or by others in the ballroom. It is this sort of thing that gives an excuse to the kill-joys who denounce dancing.

Don't insist on doing *all* the steps of the Fox-trot which you happen to know, regardless of your surroundings. Some of them may not be suited to a crowded ballroom because they take up too much room. It is inconsiderate to your fellow-dancers to indulge in these unless there is ample floor-space.

Don't be afraid to show that you are enjoying yourself. Enjoyment is what you are there for, and not to be happy in a ballroom is to admit that you are a failure. Believe me, there is nothing either distinguished or meritorious in being bored.

Don't be afraid to pay your partner some little compliment. No sensible woman cares for fulsome flattery, but every woman likes being told how nice she looks or how charmingly she dances, if there is a grain of truth in the assertion. Remember, it is up to you to make her enjoy herself. Don't miss the opportunity.

FOR THE OLD FOGEY.

Don't be a kill-joy. If you are really too tired to enjoy the dance, bed is the place for you. Don't make the youngsters feel that they are keeping you up. If you can't make yourself happy, make yourself scarce.

Don't think that the whole house is deranged because the young people have cleared the carpet and furniture out of the drawing-room for a dance. It will all be put back the next morning, and there will be one room less to spring-clean.

Don't grouse about the noise made by the young people giving a dance next door. Rather than waste time writing letters of complaint, write out a few invitations and give a dance yourself. All-round satisfaction will be the result.

Don't be for ever lamenting that there are no dances like the old dances. Remember what you in your heyday replied to the old fogeys who said the same thing about *their* young days. Nothing can stop evolution.

For the Married.

Don't give up on dancing without a struggle if you have married someone who doesn't dance. Does your husband assure you that he hates dancing? The probabilities are that he has never really given himself a chance to like it. Persuade him to try, just to please you. If he is awkward and clumsy at first, don't let him feel that he is spoiling your enjoyment. Encourage him to practise on every possible occasion. Show him that you like dancing with him. This will make

him want to dance. He will dance at
first to please you, but presently to
please himself. By the same token—

Don't be put off if your wife says she
does not care for dancing. The chances
are that it is no so much that she
dislikes dancing as that she considers
herself a bad dancer. Make her dance.
If you are tactful she will soon lose
her shyness and grow in grace. Remember that her *gaucherie* is probably
the effect of mind over matter. She
has made up her mind that dancing is
difficult and that she cannot dance.
She has, in fact, hypnotised herself
into the anti-dancing state. You can
get her out of it.

Don't insist on your wife dancing only with yourself. She may obey you, but she will either laugh at your jealousy, or resent your attitude as selfish and narrow-minded. In either case it will make her hanker after a change of partners; whereas, had you given her perfect liberty of choice, she would probably have chosen you. Conversely, don't make your husband feel that you are his dancing-partner for life. He may desire nothing better, but let him decide the matter himself.

Don't tell your husband you have nothing to wear for the dance, if you know that he can't afford to buy you a new frock. He will feel the reproach. If he is strong-minded he won't buy you the frock, and if he is weak-minded he will spend money he can't spare. In either case there will be something wrong, and neither of you will be happy. Make the best of what you have and say nothing about it.

Don't refuse to give a dance because you can't afford to give as grand a one as some of your wealthier friends. Your friends, you will find, when you come to try the experiment, will vote the cheery little informal hop just as enjoyable as the more pretentious function. As long as the company is of the right sort nothing else much matters. If the dancing is good there will be no great call upon the buffet. Don't fret because you can't give your guests champagne and *pêches Melba*. They will be perfectly happy on cider-cup and tinned pineapple.

BETWEEN DANCES.

Don't, unless you are a good talker, set the subject of conversation. Find out the topic ·in which your partner takes most interest, and listen intelligently. He, or she, will do the rest!

Don't attempt strenuous conversation. Your partner won't appreciate an exposition of the Einstein theory. She is concerned for the moment with the joy of motion, and probably doesn't care twopence for the science of it.

Don't call the waitress "Miss." It is not considered good form. A girl of my acquaintance broke off her engagement because her fiancé called the waitress "Miss." A little thing? "It's the little things that count!"

Don't, Miss Shingled, Bingled, or Bobbed, please don't comb your hair in public! It is a habit that is fast gaining ground, but it is a deplorable habit. A few minutes' reflection will, I am sure, convert you to the masculine point of view—it is a disgusting habit. A friend of mine recently informed me that he had no less than seven different samples of hair wafted on to his coat in a single evening. "But," he concluded, "when I discovered the eighth variety in my ice, it was the last straw!"

POSTSCRIPTS.

Don't be insulted if a girl offers to pay for her own ticket for a dance. The girl of the present day is naturally much more independent than her predecessors. She would rather pay her share of the evening's entertainment than rush you into something that she knows perfectly well you can't afford. And she is right.

Don't make a fuss when taxi or bus fares are being paid. There is nothing more embarrassing than the person who keeps on thrusting money upon others with noisy insistence. Either pay the fare unobtrusively, or arrange matters quietly with the other men of the party at some opportune moment. Only don't make a scene over a few pence.

Don't miss an opportunity of seeing all the best musical comedies and revues. Although it would be ridiculous to attempt the translation of most of the stage dances to the ballroom, there are many little hints on style and deportment to be picked up by watching the performances of skilled artists.

Don't be lured by the spirit of adventure into sampling an unrecognised night club. There are numerous shady establishments with high-sounding and intriguing titles that are mere shelters for the sale of intoxicating liquors during prohibited hours. There is nothing romantic or artistic about such places. They are merely rather sordid and depressing dens where the only thrill of romance is the possibility of a police-raid. Avoid them.

Don't laugh and talk noisily when the dance is over and you have come out into the public streets. Show some consideration for others less fortunate than you who have not been out enjoying themselves, and are trying to sleep. It is the disregard of such small considerations that sets certain people against dancing.

Don't allow the "muse of the many twinkling feet" to monopolise all your thoughts and energies. Never lose sight of the fact that this is merely a relaxation and not an all-absorbing interest. Otherwise you will deserve the reproach that "Good dancers have mostly better heels than heads!"

Originally published 1925
Republished 2008 by A & C Black Publishers Limited
Copyright © A & C Black, 2008
38 Soho Square, London W1D 3HB
www.acblack.com

ISBN 9781408109892

A CIP catalogue record for this book is available
from the British Library.

Printed by WKT Company Ltd, China